When hunting for JOBs, turns into a Full-Time Job

HOW TO START THE BEGINNING OF A JOB SEARCH

Ines Okanovic

STARS UNITED

STARS UNITED - Ines Okanovic   starsunited@outlook.com

Ordering Information:
Quantity sales. Special discounts are available on quantity purchases by corporations, associations, and others. For details, contact the publisher above.

Printed in Canada First

Printing: 2018 Ines Okanovic.

ISBN-13: 978-1985035607

ISBN-10: 198503560X

First Edition. Volume 1.

I want to respectfully acknowledge the Coast Salish peoples – Sḵwxwú7mesh (Squamish), Stó:lō and Səlílwətaʔ/ Selilwitulh (Tsleil-Waututh) and xʷməθkʷəy̓əm (Musqueam) Nations peoples, on whose traditional, ancestral, unceded territory, I am gratefully residing and writing from today.

With heartfelt gratitude and vast appreciation, I truly want to thank the Ministries of Social Development, WorkBC, my landlord, my loving neighbors, my wonderful Family and Relatives, my handful of my precious Friends, and my MMA community, for your undivided champion support.

We were able to overcome some very rough times, and had some very appreciable times, as well. I thank you all for always inspiring me, exactly when I felt downhearted and hopeless. Sehr viele Danke!

Words are powerless to express my gratitude to our late Mother. My gratitude for all that she had warmhearted, consistently taught us, which I today treasure ever more, is infinite. No matter the circumstances, her wonderful unconditional understanding and loving and caring dedication will forever influence my constructive growth.

Huy tseep q'u!

The connections made are not easily forgotten nor lost, and I will not forget the memories.

'uts'odelhti

I appreciate you all, and I am proud to say: We are off to great places. Our mountains are waiting, so let's get on with it!

Forget the times you have fallen,
Remember each time that you 'rose again'!
If you haven't fallen hard,
You may have not really grown then, yet.
'The future is yours', so it is said,
If you trust your Dreams, if you must then, re-invent yourself.

Good Luck in your Job Search. Don't lose your enthusiasm.
I trust you reach great achievements and never give up on yourself.

Blessed wishes, Ines Okanovic

*STARS*UNITED*

CONTENTS

INTRODUCTION

This Volume Series workbook is intended to help Job Seekers and Newly Grads with the employment exploration on: How to start a beginning of the job search.

*The Agenda in this Part 1 Volume 1 Serie, is solemnly focused on the launch of a job search.
Identify the Factors and address the Barriers that are impacting your Employment Goals.
*Use the Job Search checklists and provided assignments as a Guide and prepare yourself for your job hunt.
*Advance your Cold Calling skills and uncover your Elevator Speech by pursuing a strategic way of hunting down that specific job through these pointers found in the 'Self-Marketing' content.
*Across pursuing the strategic analysis in the 'Factors that impact' content, the *Internal and External barriers* divide themselves into your recognizable *Strengths* (enhance; build), *Weaknesses* (reduce; resolve), *Opportunities* (expand; exploit), and *Threats* (thwart; avoid).
*Identify your finds in the 'Barriers to Employment' checklist and keep track with the 'Daily Contact' and 'Job Search Tracking' sheet.

By recognizing your own barriers and developing your detailed career objective, you will be able to craft your very own job search strategy. Prepare your pen and paper for your adventure and allow this work booklet to assist you in your readiness for a focused and organized job hunt.

PREFACE

Being an active Job Seeker, my joblessness encouraged me to pursue the researching of various employment markets. That is when my curiosity flowed towards the analyzation of business performances in the lower paid wage fields. Somehow, Phys. Ed. and Arts has always been my keen interest. Consequently, I enroll to update my own skills, seeking creative ways to improve my consistent employment search, as well. Thus, has encouraged me to create this brief workbook, detailed strictly on getting prepared for that job hunt that awaits. I am affiliated with multiple vendors, local markets, and few organizations, that great networking and business relations in general, are what drove the creation of this precise text booklet. Precision was driven on the main goal to assist our strong community members in their different employment objectives.

My invested time has been solemnly focused on assisting job seekers and contractors with bridging towards an ultimate job search formula. Eventually such, is the lead towards secure success. As a sole-proprietor, I understand the struggles and the deliberate need of advancing yourself somehow, someway, further. Allow this work booklet to assist you, no matter your employment goals.

Our values do not decrease based on someone's inability to see our worth. We must either modify our Dreams, or magnify our Skills.

I do want you to succeed! Make it happen!

Blessed greetings and best wishes, Ines.

Success = Hard Work + Training + Discipline

PROLOGUE

"Pamet u glavu." -Devlisa Okanovic

(Translation: Wherever you go, no matter what the weather, always bring your own sunshine. Success is the sum of small efforts repeated day in and day out. Change what you can, accept what you can't, and be smart enough to know the difference.)

You are responsible for you.
Excuses don't provide any value.
    The best people take adversity and deal with it head on while also making it work for them. You can to that as well once you commit to this kind of mindset.
I write this stuff to help people. I hope it helps you.

ALWAYS FIND COURAGE TO REFRESH THE FOCUSING OF YOUR JOB SEARCH

TABLE OF CONTENTS

FACTORS THAT IMPACT THE JOB HUNT

If you're an active job seeker and may have spent a lot of time, searching for the "just over budget" that fits with your experience, knowledge, educational background, your skills level, etc., you're most definitely not alone. Noticing throughout certain Seasons: for many of us, the Job hunting has turned pretty much into a full-time commitment. Essentially the job search success begins with an understanding of the **FOUR MAJOR FACTORS** that impact the process itself. It took me a long time to figure out what it is I truly wanted to do career wise, in order to be a more productive member within my growing and truly strong community. Asking: How can I contribute and assist? I'd find myself frequently spending countless hours seeking for open employment positions within the classifieds, online job search sites with resume attach options, standing early in lineup at the day labor gigs, tried free-lance writing affiliate opportunities and so many other countless methods. Despite of my efforts on re-editing my CL's and creating new resume styles to advertised positions, it took me phoning the hiring managers and every so often scheduling a shadowing interview with the potential company, to find out if we may even be a good fit for one another. Frequently, unforeseen circumstances happen, and life just throws itself the way we least expect it. Therefore, it is very important to understand and recognize our own **Four Major Factors** (diagram on next page), that do play a big role in our job hunt.

"Whether you think you can or you think you can't, either way, you are right."

The Diagram below illustrates the Four Factors.

Note:Two of the factors are outside of our control (external), while the other Two are within our control (internal).

So basically, what the research comes down to, is that; The <u>external factors</u> that are outside of our control, are just as important as the <u>internal factors</u> that are within our control. By having a sound knowledge of the external factors, we can better prepare ourselves for an effective job search, at taking appropriate actions within the internal factors, that we can control.

*Keep your resume short and simple
–have LinkedIn, social media, Twitter, etc. sharpened

*Control the amount you spend on Job Boards
– focus on smaller, regional, industry related job boards and labor market information

*Create a Folder of your Job Search documents
– unite your leadership initiative, consider training your interviewing skills, be strategic

*Expect to hear a 'NO'
- start your job search sooner than later, keep building you network pipeline and practice self-awareness

BARRIERS TO EMPLOYMENT: IDENTIFY AND ADDRESS THEM

Many individuals face barriers and still manage to find success in the labor markets. Therefore, it is best to avoid operating on a prejudiced plan about 'who is', and 'who is not' employable, based on individual features, qualities, traits, etc.

Provided is a chart below to assist in resolving and identifying the Barriers to Employment. See if any appear to be of resemblance. Put a check mark to it.

[ ] Lack of Transportation, [ ] Cost of Supervision,
[ ] Concerns with lack of support system,
[ ] Fear of Interviewing, [ ] Lack of adequate nutrition,
[ ] Unrealistic job expectations,
[ ] Lack of training or education,
[ ] Gaps in employment, [ ] Ineffective job search skills,
[ ] Limited English proficiency, [ ] Long term unemployed,
[ ] Lack of appropriate clothing,
[ ] Drug/Alcohol/Substance abuse,
[ ] Criminal record, [ ] Age, [ ] Lack of self-confidence,
[ ] Lack of computer skills, [ ] Feel overwhelmed/anxious,
[ ] Fear of other people, [ ] Disability - Health problems,
[ ] Overweight / Underweight,
[ ] Family emergencies – Grieving,
[ ] Little or no work history, [ ] Suspended driver's license,
[ ] Lack of references, [ ] Lack of adequate housing

When the barriers are identified, determine how to view the situation.

Most of the time, individuals internally exaggerate. What is thought of, that is often what is mainly stopping us from finding our passion and truly living out our own purpose. And yet, if some of the barriers are just something we allow to possibly imagine, or somehow do have some legitimacy, based on unexpected and unforeseen circumstances. When such arises, there is usually a way to find solutions and perhaps try to creatively adjust our passions to work around the barriers.

Directly identifying the employer's perception of a barrier, occurs mostly during the job search. A barrier to one employer may not be a barrier to an another. It mostly depends on the goals and type of work one is experienced in. To identify the employers needs and concerns, you have to put yourself in the employer's position and think like an employer for a moment. If you're completely unsure of the expectations, it may help to contact the employer and ask them a list of prepared questions. There are few approaches to use, when it comes to addressing our barriers. Some barriers are easy to identify and resolve, while others require creativity and resourcefulness. Be that as it may, it is possible to overcome these things that block a successful employment search.

Have a positive attitude about getting help and finding work

Seek out assistance services, if you really need them to find employment. Start with looking up your local Employment Training Programs.

* Participate in rehab services, if necessary.*

Find affordable training and ways to assist in financing the courses.

Reach out to your local Community Services for help with basic needs, and for urgent Support Services, seek out your local Community Centers.

Learn how your disability can be accommodated at work.

Seek out your local Resources to help you, if you have a criminal record from being an ex-offender, or have a poor work history.

Remember that there is a tremendous amount of support and guidance

If you see that you can't overcome your barriers on your own, work with an Employment Advisor to learn about the resources and the support available to you. An Employment Advisor/ Worker can provide a well-coordinated, overall support system, in helping you find the training, maybe refer you to some counseling, and provide basic needs assistance in advising you with the fast help in order for you to find a job. With continued support in the workplace and at home. Job counselors, workforce centers, and case workers can serve as coaches and mentors to help you find out if you can get the help for your particular situation.

If you are struggling with more than one barrier, you may need to connect with different resources to help with each barrier.

The main focus must be on qualifications and positive traits, not on barriers.

If an employer asks about your barrier in a job interview, be prepared to talk about how it will not affect your ability to be a good employee:

*Identify the barrier. Sometimes the employer doesn't understand what the barrier is or how it does and does not affect your ability to work.

*Get some perspective on the barrier. Only talk about how the barrier might affect your ability to do your job or interact with people. If the barrier does not affect your job, then make sure the employer knows this.

*Come up with workable solutions and goals. Be proactive and give the employer suggestions as to how you can minimize your barrier or find ways for it to not affect your job. Talk with an employment advisor to get suggestions.

*Turn your barrier into a "selling" point.

JOB SEARCH CHECKLIST

Career Objective
[ ] I have a clear and specific career objective or objectives, which is/are
[ ] I have identified Five Companies I would like to apply to

Resume, Cover Letter & Reference Sheet
[ ] I have a completed resume specific to an employment goal
[ ] My resume has been approved/saved by the facilitator
[ ] I have a completed Cover Letter
[ ] My Cover Letter has been approved/saved by the facilitator
[ ] I have a confirmed Reference Sheet

Online / Offline Job Search Techniques
[ ] I can complete an online application
[ ] I can search for job leads using online Job Boards
[ ] I can search for companies online using a search engine

Networking
[ ] I have an Elevator Speech I am comfortable using
[ ] I can use my Contact Sheet to keep track of the jobs I am applying for
[ ] I know how to drop off my resumes for an advertised or unadvertised job
[ ] I have a list of at least five companies I would like to apply to

Email and Voicemail
[ ] I have an email account and I know how to attach my resume and cover letter
[ ] I can write a short greeting via email to potential employers and others
[ ] I have a voicemail message that is professional enough to an employer

Interviews
[ ] I feel confident answering the five common and difficult questions
[ ] I have appropriate interview clothes

FOCUSING ON YOUR CAREER OBJECTIVE

Career Objectives

      *An objective tells potential employers the sort of work you are hoping to do
      *Short and Sweet is preferred
      *Simple, Clear, and Concise
      *Indicates specific position for which you are applying for
      *If you're aiming for career fairs, objectives should be general or removed
      *Be specific about the job you want to apply for

For example: To be an active member of a productive society and to utilize my knowledge and experience for the service of humanity in general and my country in particular under the supervision of a well-reputed organization in a challenging environment.

CAREER OBJECTIVES:	**TARGETING COMPANIES:**
Plan A - most desired objective	-most valuable employer
Plan B - alternative objective	-most valuable alternative company
Plan C - alternative objective	-alternative company

What do you consider your strengths towards these objectives?

Is there anything that you lack as a qualification towards these objectives?

It is very important to learn job hunting techniques. Some are:

Networking Skills: writing and practicing an elevator speech, dropping off resumes in person for an advertised or unadvertised position, networking during workshops and deep research within the hidden job market, making a cold call, filling out a contact sheet, attending seminars, workshops, job fairs

Online Job Search Skills: reviewing the Job Search list, finding job postings online - Job Boards, emailing your resumes and cover letters, researching a company online, completing an online application, email a follow up

Quick Facts: **80-85% of all jobs are never advertised!**
At least 60% -some report even higher statistics! Most jobs are found by networking.
These Jobs are called the Hidden Job Market.
Many people put 80% of their effort on 20% of the opportunities!

The way to tap into the hidden job marked is suggested to be mostly through networking. Many job seekers are unable to network. Some just ignore networking as a job search tool and as a result, find their job search lengthy and challenging. There are many tools we can use to access these hidden opportunities. If you're interested in giving networking a try, beware that it is about building new relationships and utilizing the relationships you have already developed. **Networking is not about asking for a job or expecting immediate employment.** The key to successful networking is to put the energy needed into making it work.

Get yourself organized with a business card file or written list of positive and productive people. Remember to stay in contact through regular phone calls, emails and holiday greetings. Start setting goals for yourself, such as five new contacts per week. Be ready to create your own Network.

It is very worthwhile to create a marketing pitch. A short description of what you have to offer. Write down a few of your features. Then for each one, state the advantages of those features and the benefits of having someone on staff with those specified advantages. Employers are interested in the benefits offered to them, which arises from the features and advantages stated below:

FEATURE	STRENGTHS	ADVANTAGE TO EMPLOYER
Example: Number of years of experience	5yrs of experience	Excellent driving record Very familiar w/local roads Aware of safety procedures
Delivery Driver w/Class5 DL	Focused in my career as a Delivery Driver	Committed to this career Would be a stable, long term employee, willing to learn new skill
Skills	Good verbal, written, communication skills, effective listening skills, and organizational skills	Interacts with customers and staff in a courteous and professional manner

Skills	Performs circle check of vehicles and maintains truck log book	Care in the overall safety and maintenance of the vehicles
Personal Attributes	Able to work independently with limited supervision	Trustworthy with good judgement in making decisions

Practice your Objectives! Try to put it on a paper together for yourself. Identifying your own features, strengths, and the advantages you bring to Employers. When working constantly on this continuous process, you will eventually maintain your professionalism and be more organized in your job hunt. By receiving a little more clarity, you can eliminate a lot of barriers and are assured of what you bring to the table at the end of the day. Wheater it is production, profits, promotion or overtime, you will be able to identify the benefits you bring to employers.

Which brings us to the next discussion:

SELF-MARKETING (THE ELEVATOR SPEECH).

SELF-MARKETING
"The Elevator Speech"

Another tool in your marketing binder should include the Elevator Speech. It is namely titled because it can be said in the time it approximately takes to travel one floor in an elevator ~about 45 seconds.

Sample Elevator Speech for a TV News Anchor

I have a diverse background so let me tell you about the best project I worked on: I joined a show that had lackluster ratings and no social media presence. I used my experience producing and hosting national TV programs, along with my on-air anchoring and reporting skills, to engage the audience before, during and after the show. Produce an increase with the audience and in ratings, and make a 10% improvement in the operating budget. My name is Joe Doe and I make TV news shows profitable.

<u>Start by listing your strengths, qualities and attributes.</u> Write up your experiences, your education, your skills, and your strengths. Then arrange it into a powerful elevator speech. Elevator Speeches and FAB *(Features Advantages Benefits)* statements are very versatile. Use them when you meet people, or go to events, as the answers to interview questions and for your cold calls. You can modify them to fit almost any situation, evidently.

When cold calling, make sure you target the company - *"I am phoning your company in regards to."*.

And instead of ending with, *"Do you know of anyone who could use my skills?"*, you could end with: *"When may I swing by and meet the team / you?"*

"COLD CALLING"

Next to Public Speaking, **Cold Calling** might be very daunting. Some people try to avoid cold calling at all costs. It can also be a very constructive, yet still a lost method for career-minded individuals. Let's try to separate ourselves from the other job searchers, who don't think about doing any cold calling.

So, a 'Cold Call' is basically when you call someone on the phone (that person is not expecting your call at all), for the purpose of getting that person to assist you with something.

After introducing yourself during a recruiting cold call and ensuring yourself that the recruit is in a position where they can speak freely, you need to answer this critical question: *"Why are you calling me?"*

In order to 'lock down' a potential employer and add them to your interviews list, you will need to navigate the first phone call. Therefore, please keep in mind to be pleasant to the 'Gatekeeper' and give information to get information. Blind cover letter can be the decision maker.

Sales people use cold calling to introduce themselves directly towards potential sales prospects, in the hopes that this person will buy something from them.

Recruiters use cold calling to find companies who will let them work on jobs that they are trying to fill. Some employers also use cold calling to find job candidates for the jobs that they're working on.

You can use **cold calling** to speak with potential hiring managers towards enquiring about jobs with their company. Though probably shouldn't just call and ask companies randomly if they have any openings. That will make you look like an unmotivated and not well-prepared job seeker. However, in your calls to various human resources departments, ask for the names and titles of hiring managers as well as the contact information for human resources decision makers. Organize your calling campaign to make the most of your time. Create a spreadsheet with columns for contact information and names. Verify email addresses, postal mail addresses and telephone numbers. And always get correct spellings and pronunciation for people's names. Cold calling 50 people on the phone is obviously more effective than visiting 50 companies in person, but cold calling is one of the hardest – and most maligned – tactics that people use, to get what they want. Mostly, it's stated because cold calling has so many negative stereotypes associated with it:

*It's scary to do

*It uses scripted, forced conversations that sound like a sales pitch

*The fear of being rejected or not knowing what to say

Cold calling is not easy but it doesn't have to be difficult either. Plus, because the vast majority of people who are looking for the same jobs you are, will not cold call employers. You can use it to separate yourself from them.

The best way to approach cold calling is to have a plan of attack before you pick up the phone. Research suggests against any scripting of your calls, because you don't want to sound like you are reading from a script. Nor can you actually predict exactly what the person you will speak with, will actually say. But if you have little or no experience with cold calling, what you might want to do is write out a marketing message that you will use for your cold calling. Refer to that message when the hiring manager answers the phone. Some job seekers are reluctant about calling human resources departments for names and contact information of employees who are in charge of hiring. Getting the information is all in the way you ask. Since you're essentially asking the gatekeeper to do you a favor, be pleasant and give information to get information.

For example, when you call say, "Hello, my name is ... and I've read so many great things about working for your company in this month's ... magazine / web- blog. I'd like to send my resume to the human resources manager. Would you please give me his or her full name and contact information?"

A suitable goal of a cold call for a job searcher is to get a relevant hiring manager on the phone and to get them to agree to meet with, at their office. In other words, <u>you want to get an interview</u>. **To get an interview you will need to illustrate to the hiring manager that you are someone who solves a problem that they have, and that you are in fact the ideal person to solve that problem.** Cold calling requires a strategy. Select companies to approach, based on some factors. For example: based on the industry, their employee base or size, the geographical area or any other factors important to your job search. Comparatively, companies recognized for helping employees achieve work-life balance. <u>Start with a telephone call</u>, but don't end there. <u>Follow through with a letter</u> to the human resources or hiring manager. <u>In your blind cover letter, ask for an informational interview</u> if you don't want to risk being turned down for an interview for a job that doesn't exist. An informational interview gets your foot in the door and in front of the reader, so you can make personal impression. If the reader doesn't meet you personally, ask for your resume to be kept on file for future consideration.

<u>Another effective strategy is to use postal mail instead of email, for your correspondence.</u> So many job seekers use email, a regular-mail application package stands out among the rest. Doing these things will help you be more active and take more action towards your goals. Taking the initiative to go on informational interviews, further develops your skills and abilities. Also, actively networking can help you with developing the evolution of your career path, as you seek new opportunities! <u>Get started with the next step in your job hunt by giving Cold Calling a try.</u> Although each call will roll out differently, here are the main points you want to cover during the call:

*Opening introduction: *briefly introduce yourself with enthusiasm, i.e..: "Hi, this is John Smith." Don't bother asking a question like "How are you" or "Is this a good time to talk", because it just gives the person a chance to get you off the phone.*

*Give a brief explanation of your work background and your level of experience. *i.e.. "I'm a Database Administrator with 5 years of hands-on experience and I'm contacting you to enquire about your requirements for someone with my skillset."*

*Then follow up with something exceptional and specific that makes you stand out from other candidates. *i.e.. "I am certified on Database Platform A and B and in my most recent position, reduced database downtime by 23%."*

<u>It should be good to pop in a quick reference to the fact that you're a job searcher, without specifically asking for a job</u>. At this point all you are trying to do is get in front of them for an interview. That's the goal of the call. <u>You don't want to put the person off, by coming right out and asking for a job</u>. But at the end of the day, that's your ultimate goal! There is no sense in beating around the bush and making it seem like you're calling them to have a chat. You made

the call for a purpose and that purpose is to let them know why they need to interview you.
*Ask for an interview. *i.e.. "When can I meet with you in person?"*

Again, these three points may only form part of the cold call because it will really depend on what the person on the other end of the phone says in response. However, those three points are the main ones you want to get across during the call. *So now that you've got your script ready, you need hiring managers to speak with.*

The best thing to do is to *make a list of companies* who are advertising for people *with your skills or short of that*, to make a list of companies whichever you know need people with your skills from time to time. Perhaps you have friends who work for companies that might need your skills and they could put the good word in for you with the hiring manager before you call.

Prior to you start making your calls, *ensure that you keep track of all companies and the contact details for hiring managers you speak with*, so you can effectively manage your list. <u>You don't want to speak with someone twice and forget that you've already spoken with them.</u> Putting an Excel spreadsheet together will help keep track of your progress.

If the hiring manager won't meet with you – and many will try to avoid this, especially if they don't have a job opening currently – they might try to get you off the phone by asking for your resume instead. <u>If you can't get an interview and have exhausted your options for arranging one, you might agree to email your resume to them for future consideration.</u>

Finally, <u>don't be disappointed with rejection</u>. You might get rejected more often than not, but effectively cold calling the hiring managers has better odds than simply firing off an equal number of emails and waiting for the calls to come in. A growing and healthy professional network is invaluable, so be sure that you're making an effort to go to networking events and join in on groups like Meetups. Often, these networking events will also include a panel discussion or talks with thought leaders in your field. Take these chances to listen to innovative ideas, learn about the latest trends, and have engaging discussions. The people you meet at these events and in these groups will also likely be highly interested in your field and dedicated to improving themselves. These are the types of people you want to meet and connect with! <u>You never know when a new job opportunity will arise</u>, so it's important to build a strong network and show your new connections that you're passionate about your field.

Doing these simple facts, will help you be more active and take more action towards your goals. Taking the initiative to go on informational interviews, further developing your skills and abilities, and actively networking, can help with the first step towards an upgraded evolution of your career path, as you seek new opportunities. There are always latest opportunities to refresh and develop your skills with. Regardless of whether or not you're currently working, you can do things as volunteering, teaching yourself, and working on personal projects. Doing these things shows potential employers your initiative and drive to keep improving, and they can also help you fill gaps in your employment history. Seek out to your local organizations that may need your skills – this can include anything from accounting to building service working to construction. Many non-profits and charities are looking for help in various roles. Therefore, volunteering can help you add to your experience, while supporting your local community in assisting their great causes! You may also add more skills to your skills, on your own time, through self-guided learning and working on side projects.

There are many resources available to you to help you learn more about your field – from websites, along with online courses, via videos, and books. Read up and put your new knowledge to use and walk the walk by working on a personal or side project and confidently continue job hunting for that specific dream job of yours. Along the way, build yourself your own portfolio with stated worksheets and copies of practice samples provided in the assignments you create for yourself with your to-do sheets available for your convenience. There are great ways to expand your network while learning more about the industry, company, or specific role you're looking to get into. Often, people will be more receptive when you're simply looking to learn and gather more information, than when you're asking them for a JOB (just over budget).

Go through the connections you've made in the past. See if there's anyone whose wits you'd like to pick, over a coffee. Maybe someone in your network can even introduce you to a contact at your dream company! LinkedIn can be great for this, as you're able to see the mutual connections you have with a person. In addition to helping you make new connections, informational interviews can help you narrow down what you want to do, by getting a better sense of what to expect of the company or the position you're considering. This is especially helpful for us students, the new grads, and those who are looking to make the jump into a new industry or advanced role.

Persistence is the one of the keys.

CREATE YOUR SCRIPT HERE:

1) Opening introduction

Who Am I?

Give some context for who you are and in regards to why you are calling. Introduce yourself using your first and last names, immediately. Employers do not like phone calls from nameless strangers. After you introduce yourself, tell the employer what you need. Don't expect her/him to guess the reason for your call. Be specific but tactful in stating your desire for a position.

Could mention your student status, the year, what program and how you obtained the individual's name or where you met him/her.

What are some of your interests, strong skills, your experiences or specific goals as they concern to the job/organization/field you are interested in?

What makes you unique and worthy of getting to know?

2) Give a brief explanation of your work-background and your levels of experiences, your education and extra study credits if applicable. Your interest and knowledge of the company. That brief explanation could become your lead statement or a good closing statement. It is a brief statement of your main qualifications: your number of years of experience, your education and your main skills. This is what 'hooks' the potential employer's interest and will surely set you apart from other applicants.

What Have I Done / What Can I Do?

What notable or relevant accomplishments, skills, assets, experience or educational achievements do you have?
Something exceptional and specific, that makes you stand out.

3) Ask for an Interview

If your goal is to meet with the employer, then suggest that, *"May I come in for an interview at your convenience?"*, or, *"Would it be possible to meet with you sometime this week/next week/tomorrow/this afternoon?"*, *"I would really appreciate the opportunity to meet with you. Would Monday morning or Wednesday afternoon be better for you?"*. *"I'd really enjoy the opportunity of presenting myself in person and giving you a copy of my updated resume."*.

If the answer is no, ask if you can send a resume or come in to fill out an application form. You might also ask if they know of anyone else who is looking for someone with your qualifications. You may also ask when a good time would be to drop off your resume.

What Do I Want?

*What is the purpose for your communication with the individual?

*What information or action would you like from the individual you are contacting?

Three possible requests include:

*To follow up on an application – *"I am calling to follow up on the posi tion of Marketing Assistant, to which I sent my application in by e-mail on July 1st. I'm really interested in this position and was just wondering if you received my application and where you are right now in the hiring process."*

*To ask about job openings (cold call) – *"I was wondering if you might know of any openings for qualified servers right now at The Underground or anywhere else on campus."*

*To request advice and information – *"I was wondering if I could come meet with you for 10 to 15 minutes, to ask for some advice and information on how to gain entry into the field of marketing."*

Practice your cold calling script any chance you get! Once you have your solid script ready, you need hiring managers to speak with.

PHONE SCRIPT FOR COLD CALLING

CALLER: "May I please have the name of the   "

Or "May I please speak to   " (when name is known)

RECEPT: "What is this regarding?" (Receptionist may screen you)

CALLER: "   " (When the Hiring Manager is on the phone with you, be prepared to talk about the four parts of a Phone Script, including your well-pitched 30 second "elevator speech")

Name: "Hello, my name is   , I appreciate you taking my call."

Or "   "

Position: "I am interested in   "

Or "I'm calling to   "

Hook:

Goal:

COLD CANVASSING – HAVE A PURPOSE

Email
*Make sure you have the right email address
*Write an introduction letter in the body of the email and attach your resume
*Follow up with a phone call

Phone
*Ask for the HR Manager (know the person's name)
*Write down questions you have before you make the call
*Introduce yourself
*State why you are contacting them
*Give details about yourself
*Ask how you can forward on further information for upcoming employment
*Thank them for taking the time to talk with you

Face to Face
*Be presentable
*Confident and Assertive and Alert
*Show interest
*Open and comfortable Body Language
*Be clear and precise

MOVING CLOSER TO YOUR EMPLOYMENT GOAL

Assignments:

1) *Finding a job posting to apply to*. There are three ways to find a posting that is suitable to your background: an online posting, a posting from a company's Career page, a posting from the JD (Job Developer) List. Choose a posting and print it out if possible, or save it as a printable file, or take a picture of it, or write it down in your spreadsheet log. This will be the basis for your targeted resume and cover letter; your email assignment and the focus of your interview practice.

a) Choose a posting from the JD job list that meets your qualifications and which you are interested in applying to.

b) Research the company and complete the Company Research paper.

c) Write a targeted cover letter and resume for that position. Write the cover letter to the attention of the Job Developer overseeing that position. Your Facilitator will supply you with the JD's name

And / Or

a) Find an online job posting that is related to your Career Objective(s). Print it out.

b) Research the company and complete the Company Research paper.

c) Target your resume and cover letter for this position

And / Or

Have you identified any companies you wish to target for your job search?

a) Research these companies to see if there is a posting on their Career page. Print it out.

b) Complete the Company Research paper

c) Target your resume and cover letter for that position

2) *Email your resume and cover letter to your facilitator*, as the employer:
 *Include your resume and cover letter as attachments
 *Include a short message in the body of the email

*In the subject line of the email: Application for the _____ position
*Address: _____ (your local employment agency)

3) *Apply online to a job* at Subway (or other company you wish to apply to)

BIGGEST CAREER MISTAKES

*Assuming that you know everything
*Forgetting to Network
*Not being prepared for meetings
*Ignoring the value of business cards
*Engaging in office drama
*Arriving to meetings late
*Being satisfied doing the minimum
*Not reading up on your industry
*Forgetting to make a LinkedIn page
*Over-sharing personal stories at work
*Burning bridges when leaving a job
*Dressing unprofessionally
*Not proof-reading your emails
*Not seeing the value in entry-level positions
*Not learning from your mistakes and failures
*Failing to seek out a mentor
*Being a negative person
*Forgetting to thank people who help you
*Not asking for help when you need it
*Not standing up for what you're worth

COMPANY RESEARCH NOTES

JOB OPPORTUNITY
Job Title You're Interviewing for:
Date / Time of the Interview:

COMPANY INFORMATION
Company Name:
Address:
Phone Number:
Website:

*Review the company website — in particular, the "About" page, "Media" section (if there is one), and information about their products and services.
*Check out the source code on the company website to see if there are particular keywords that

give insight to the company's focus. (Go to the company website. In your web browser, go to the "View" menu and choose "View Source.") Note: Not all companies include this information in their source code (look at the title code and meta tags).

   Describe the company (Is it a subdivision of another company? How many employees? How many locations? What industry? Structure — public, private, family-owned, nonprofit, etc.)

Facebook business page: www.facebook.com/

   Look at the content the company posts, but also look at what other people post on the company's page. Can you identify any potential problems that need solving?

Company Twitter handle: @
Blog URL:

   Review the blog for greater insight into the company.
YouTube channel: www.youtube.com/
   Take a look at the official videos posted by the company.
   Also, do a search for the company on YouTube and see if there are any videos posted by employees, the media, or affiliates.

Notes / Thoughts based on online profile research:

GOOGLE

   1) Google search the company. Review the first three pages of Google results — anything interesting?
   Notes:

   2)*Look at what other job postings are open at the company* — these can help you identify growth opportunities within the company.

   3) *Do a Google news search on the company* (news.google.com).
Any news stories? Any major announcements in the last 18 months?

LINKEDIN, INDEED, JOB SEARCH ENGINES

Search "Companies" on Job Search Engines

   Does the company have a profile on LinkedIn?   Yes   No

   How many followers does the company have on its company page? If the company has a profile, does it list their,

Company type:
Company size:
Industry:
Year founded:
Headquarters (location):
Makeup of employees (location, job title, education):

If the company has provided "Company Updates," be sure to read those.

On the company's LinkedIn page, click the yellow "Follow" button, and information about the company will be included in your "Updates" feed on the home page of your LinkedIn profile

THE INTERVIEWER

You can often find this information on LinkedIn, Facebook, or through a Google search.

Whom are you interviewing with?

If the interviewer is a technical manager, have they written any LinkedIn Recommendations for current or previous employees? What skills/attributes did they value?

COMPETITIVE ANALYSIS

Who is the company's biggest competitor?
Website:

Strengths/Weaknesses/Opportunities/Threats (SWOT) Analysis

STRENGTHS *(compared to the competitor, what is the prospective employer's greatest strengths in the market):*
WEAKNESSES:
OPPORTUNITIES:
THREATS:

UNDERSTANDING THE POSITION

Who does this position report to (name and job title):

Do any employees report to this position (names and job titles):

What are the top three challenges of the job?

1.

2.

3.

Which "employer buying motivators" apply to this position?

Make money,   Save money,   Save time,   Make work easier,

Solve a specific problem, Be more competitive, Expand business,

Attract new customers,

Build relationships / maintain an image,

Retain existing customers

Based on salary research, I would expect this position to pay between:

$ and $.

<u>PERSONAL ASSESSMENT</u>

What is my biggest strength/qualification for this position?

What sets me apart from other candidates?

What might keep me from getting the job?

What question do you least want to be asked in this interview?

Why do you want to work for this company?

EMAILING REFRESHER NOTES

The whole process of modern job hunting has shifted online, with plenty of platforms and apps available for the average job seeker. And since this move of "everything online" is still a pretty new thing, many of us are starting to understand why the job emails that some of us have been sending out, appear…. troubled, to say the least.

The job emails are NOT the kind of emails we should be sending. Not only will you not get the job, but you'll probably sour that particular employer to any future applications you send their way. *It states that those who don't learn from history, are doomed to repeat it.* So here is a list of problematic emails that current research shows, on how employers actually have received such emails before, and an explanation as to why they are not good for the job prospects. *Email's sample below are only recreations, unless otherwise stated, because we don't want to hurt any feelings.*

What sets me apart from other candidates?"

Sample Email #1

Ellia Pikri <ellia.pikri@gmail.com>
to employer-senpai, ellia.pikri ⌄

Hello there,

I am attaching my CV for any open positions

Regards,
Ellia

<Narrator voice> but that CV was never attached…

Truly a tragic mistake. This mistake is especially unforgivable now that Gmail actually notifies you if you forget to add attachments (try to send an email that says 'attached' without attaching anything and confirm that there is alert for missing attachments).

It's especially egregious if what you're forgetting is the CV. The Curriculum Vitae is that what should, ideally, convince the employer on why you ought to be hired. Not to mention, (as you can see in that Sample Email#1) it doesn't really provide much detail. Employers are usually very busy people, and they have no time to scour through the (nonexistent) resume to figure out what job you're even trying to apply for.

Tips on how to avoid few common mistakes:

a) *Prepare a template email in your drafts with all of the basics already attached and written-out. (i.e. the initial greeting and the CV attached)*

b) *Include some sentences that explain why you are the candidate for the position you're applying for. Ideally, the second part in the body of your email message should be uniquely directed to each and every new email. Focus on the different aspects of the job, like the job-scope and how you can uniquely contribute to the company without forgetting the basics.*

c) Be proactive! _State clearly what job you're looking for._ _If you think you suit more than one job, point out all of them in the email, within reason of course. Don't indicate six different jobs. Rather, show that you're decisive, but also that you've done at least some research on the company and know what the company is looking for._

The important thing about writing that first email, or that cover letter, is to introduce your personality! Make sure that it's professional, but don't forget to make it interesting.

If you've done volunteer work at the bottom of the ocean to benefit orphan fishes or something, that's definitely something that has to be somewhere (be it in your resume or email body). If not, let your personality shine through from your writing style.

Even indicating that you're a die-hard fan of the Barenaked Ladies. In a retrospect, as long as it's done in a formal format and with a touch of class, it can make your application stand out from others, surely.

When you are job searching, you will likely use the email for a number of reasons. You might send an email asking about some job openings, or email out your cover letter with the resume attached. You might send networking emails, asking contacts for help with your job search. Possibly also try to remember to send out your 'thank you' email messages after the interviews. When you are using the email to job search, it's important that all your communications are as professional as they would be if you were writing an old-fashioned paper letter. Below is a little bit more detailed information on all that a job searcher needs to know about 'job search email etiquette'. Including, what to put in your job search emails, how to format your emails, and how to make sure your email messages are read.

EMAIL ETIQUETTE TIPS FOR JOB SEEKERS

Use a professional email account. Make sure you have an email account name that is appropriate for business use, e.g. firstname.lastname@gmail.com. There are a variety of free web-based email accounts, like Gmail, Hotmail and Yahoo, that you can use. It also makes sense to set up an email account just for job searching, so your professional email doesn't get mixed in with your personal mail.

Send your email to a specific person. When possible, send your email to a contact person, rather than a general email box. Send a copy to yourself, so you have a record of the emails you have sent and the jobs you have applied to.

Use a clear subject line. Your email message needs a subject line. If you leave the subject blank, the email is probably going to end up in a spam mailbox or be deleted. Make sure you list the position you are applying for in the subject line of your email message, so the employer is clear as to what job you are applying for. You might want to include your name in the subject as well.

Below are two examples of appropriate subject lines:

Subject Line: Communications Director Position
Subject Line: Marketing Associate Position / Your Name

Choose a simple font. Avoid ornate, difficult-to-read fonts. Use a basic font like Times New Roman, Arial, or Cambria. Don't use color in your text, neither. Use size 10 or 12 point, so that the email is easy to read, without being too big.

Write, like it's a business letter. In general, your email messages should look a lot like business letters. They should include words, not acronyms nor slang nor emoticons. They should be written in full sentences and paragraphs. Begin with a salutation, and end with a send-off and your signature (brief well wishes, with your name and contact information followed as a closing). The only difference between an email and a business letter is that in an email you do not need to include the employer's contact information, the date, and your information in the top left corner.

Keep it brief. People tend to skim, or even ignore, very long emails. Keep your email brief and to the point. (KISS it: keep it short and simple)

Include a signature. Include an email signature with your contact information, so it's easy for the hiring manager to get in touch with you. Including a link to your LinkedIn profile is a good way to give the hiring manager more information on your skills and abilities.

Below is a sample email signature:

First Name   Last Name
Email Address
Phone/Cell Phone
LinkedIn Profile (Optional)
Email Message Content

If you do have a contact person, address your email to "Dear Mr. /Ms. Last Name". If you don't, address your email to "Dear Hiring Manager", or simply start with the first paragraph of your message.

When you're applying for a job via email, copy and paste your cover letter into the email message or write your cover letter in the body of the email message.

If the job posting asks you to send your resume as an attachment, send your resume as a PDF or a Word document.

No matter your purpose for emailing, be clear about why you are writing and the purpose of your email message. Include this information *early on in the email.*

CHOOSE POSITIVITY
DEFAULT TO TRANSPARENCY
FOCUS ON SELF-IMPROVEMENT
BE A NO-EGO DOER
LISTEN FIRST, THEN LISTEN MORE
COMMUNICATE WITH CLARITY
MAKE TIME TO REFLECT
LIVE SMARTER, NOT HARDER
SHOW GRATITUDE
DO THE RIGHT THING

ASSIGNMENTS TEMPLATE:

Find a job posting to apply to:
Choose a posting from JD list
Research the Company
Write a targeted cover letter and resume
 And / Or
Finding related posting online:
Find related career objectives online
Research the Company
Target your resume and cover letter
And / Or
Spotted any companies you wish to select?:
Research those companies
Complete the Company Research paper
Target your resume and cover letter for those positions

Email your resume/cl to your facilitator:
Include your resume and cover letter
Include a short message
Address the subject line and information

Apply online to a job you wish to apply to
Attach your resume and include your CL and CV
KISS your message index
Address the subject line and precise information

RELATED IDEAS

Digital Elevator Pitch,   Join Professional Associations,
Digital Business Card,   Volunteer - Community Service,
Create a Blog,   Attend Seminars,
Attend Webinars,   Join a Professional "Group",
Video Blogging,   "Like" Something,
Request Recommendations, Join an Alumni "Group",
Round-Table Opportunities, Engage / Comment Online

Infographic Summary

Donate Your Skills

DAILY CONTACT SHEETS

Job Application Record

Job Title	Company Name/ Website	Contact Name/Title	Phone/ Fax/ E-mail	Mailing Address	Resume Sent (Date)	How Sent	References Sent	Job Description/ Keywords	Application Status/ Date	Interview/ Date

Job Search Tracking Sheet

	Company	Position	Contact	Date 5ent/ Contacted	Resume	Cover Letter	Other	My Action/ Follow-up
Example:	Caterpillar	Marketing Intern	Joe Smith	1/10/2007	YES	Yes		Call Joe on 1/21/07 to check status

CV UPDATES
Refresh CV content
Improve Cover Letter
Review References
Proofread and error check
Refine work experiences
Consider design changes
Update social profiles

COMMUNITY WORK
Volunteer your time to a Charity
Research different industry requirements
Undertake part-time work
Research networking events
Get involved in community projects
Global Voluntary Work

SKILL SET
Gap analyze your content skill set
Take a FREE online course
Join a Summer workshop
Discover a new hobby
Read industry related books for inspiration

PREPARATION FOR POST SUMMER
Review courses on new academic year
Sign up for email job alerts
Enlist the help of a recruitment agency

COMMIT 30-40 HOURS PER WEEK
(UNTIL GOAL IS REACHED)

<u>15 Touches per day:</u>
o Five Applications
o 10 reach-outs or follows-ups
o 1-2 Informational Interview Requests

<u>2 Networking Events per week:</u>
Network for food, jobs, mentors, industry info, workshops, seminars, etc.

<u>Practice Five Hours per week:</u>
Spend your time productively on whatever you need
o Algorithms
o Behavioral Interview Questions
o Technical Interview Questions
o Company & Industry Research

<u>1 Check-In per week:</u>
o Communicate an update to a trusted advisor or your accountability partner, to ensure you do stay on track
o Solicit Feedback and Evaluation at least once a month

Job Title, Company Name / Website, Contact Name / Title,
Phone / Fax / Email, Mailing address, Resume sent / Date, Sent
how? (email, in person, mail), References Sent, Job description,
KeywordsApplication Status, Interview / Date

www.ingramcontent.com/pod-product-compliance
Lightning Source LLC
Chambersburg PA
CBHW081645220526
45468CB00009B/2563